THE OFFICIAL

LIVERPOOL

CENTENARY YEARBOOK

THE OFFICIAL LIVERPOOL CENTENARY YEARBOOK

STAN LIVERSEDGE

Foreword by MARK WRIGHT

HAMLYN

First published in 1992

Hamlyn is an imprint of Reed Consumer Books
Michelin House, 81 Fulham Road London SW3 6RB
part of Reed International Books Ltd

Copyright © Reed International Books Limited 1992

Book Design: Four Corners

ISBN 0 600 57688 4

Pnnted in Great Britain

Photographic Acknowledgements

Front cover. Main picture – Sporting Pictures (UK) Ltd,
Inset picture – Colorsport.

Back cover; Top right – AllSport/Steve Morton;
Below – Colorsport.

All other photographs are by John Cocks/Photographique
except for the following: AllSport, p5, p36, pp40-41, p53;
AllSport/Steve Morton, p9, p35; AllSport/Chris Cole, p29;
AllSport/Steve Botterill, p42.

Foreword

It was easy for me when Liverpool asked me to sign; I have relatives who live on Merseyside, and Anfield has long been my favourite ground even if I had never been on a winning side here. At Southampton Kevin Keegan used to tell us that Anfield was the place for football and atmosphere, saying, "Let's go out and enjoy it!"

Everyone knows how often Liverpool have been winners, but 1992 was the first time in five attempts that I had ever got passed the semi-finals of a major Cup competion. At White Hart Lane in 1986, I also suffered a broken leg; then there was that agonising World Cup penalty shoot-out.

THE WAITING GAME

In this year's FA Cup semi-final replay against Portsmouth, I was lucky enough to win the toss to choose ends for the spot kicks, so I chose the end where our fans were massed, and also the toss to decide the order. Remembering that England went first and lost, I decided to play the waiting game; it worked and we were off to Wembley. In the League, I honestly believe that, but for our injuries, we would have finished much closer to Leeds and Manchester United.

WEMBLEY GLORY

The highlight of my club career, however, came on 9 May when I led Liverpool in the final at Wembley and, after beating Sunderland, it was fantastic to walk up the famous steps to collect the FA Cup. The whole day was a great experience. As you go through this book and recall the events of season 1991-92, I am sure that you'll be looking forward to greater things in season 1992-93. My hope is that we will live up to the expectations of our supporters, and in saying this, I know that I'm speaking for everybody at Anfield; we all want to be winners. In the meantime, I hope you get a real kick out of reading the Liverpool Centenary Yearbook.

Mark Wright

THE NEW KEMLYN STAND, due to be opened in August 1992, takes shape.

ALL CHANGE AT

Throughout their 100-year history – March 15, 1992 was the centenary anniversary – Liverpool Football Club have rarely, if ever, known such a time of change, on and off the pitch.

Graeme Souness became manager near the end of season 1990-91, and injuries made his first year fraught with problems. Liverpool dealt freely on the transfer market. For just over £8M, in came: Dean Saunders, Mark Wright, Mark Walters, Rob Jones, Michael Thomas, and Istvan Kozma. Liverpool received over £5M for: Steve Staunton, Gary Gillespie, Peter Beardsley, David Speedie, Jimmy Carter, Steve McMahon and Gary Ablett, and Glenn Hysen was allowed to go on a free transfer.

During the turbulent season, Graeme Souness asserted: "This is a monstrous job. My predecessors have achieved so much that if we don't win something each season, the manager is bound to be regarded as a failure. I accept that there must be a fear – I prefer to call it an apprehension – of failing. Never write us off. You dismiss Liverpool at your peril."

CHANGES OFF THE FIELD TOO!

There were developments behind the scenes, too, as Liverpool acquired a new chairman and Bob Paisley, after almost 53 years at Anfield, bowed out. David Moores, the 46-year-old nephew of ex-Everton chairman, Sir John Moores, took over from Noel White as chairman. Aged four, he had been taken to Anfield by his father, Cecil, and he soon became proud to be numbered among the Koppites. David, whose Mercedes car bears the registration plate KOP 1, said: "I count myself a fan. I've been on the board only 18 months, but my ambition was to become chairman."

The redevelopment of Anfield meant £2M was needed and Moores stepped in. Chief executive Peter Robinson explained: "He has taken a substantial block of the rights issue, and that is being used towards financing the Kemlyn Road stand. All the fans will benefit directly from David's investment in the club."

Liverpool's new image extends to the kit, as for season 1992-93 there will be a new sponsor's name on the famous red shirts; the Candy logo will be replaced by one known world-wide: Carlsberg, the lager brewers.

⚽ THE LIVERPOOL TEAM of 1893-4, modelling their kit ...

⚽ ... AND ROB JONES and David Burrows, modelling the 1992-93 kit.

the jones boy

⚽ **IT'S BACK TO CREWE** for Rob, but as a Liverpool player, just before the FA Cup tie.

It could be a company name: Platt, Thomas & Jones. In a way, it is, because David Platt, Geoff Thomas and Rob Jones all played for Crewe Alexandra and won full international caps with England.

GRESTY ROAD

In the Jones boy, Liverpool reckon they've landed a chip off the old block – because his grandad, Bill, played 278 times for the Anfield club, as well as winning a couple of England caps.

Rob Jones went to a rugby playing school in Ellesmere Port, a town on the Wirral, but though he played rugby there, Rob played soccer on Sundays for Ellesmere Port Youth Centre, and one memorable game for another side called Holton Boys. Memorable, because it led to Crewe. In fact, the game was against Crewe, and two of the specators were Crewe manager Dario Gradi and his then youth-team coach Barry Bennell. Crewe decided Rob was worth a trial.

FROM GRESTY ROAD TO OLD TRAFFORD

After having played his first game for Crewe at 16, he played his last match for the Gresty Road club in September 1991. Later in the week, Rob (by now aged 20) answered a call from Dario Gradi. "He asked whether I'd like to play for Liverpool against Manchester United on Sunday. I was shaking when he said Graeme Souness wanted to speak to me." But play against United the Jones boy did. It was a debut which won universal praise, and the bouquets have been flying ever since.

Things happened fast, after that

£300,000 transfer to Liverpool: the debut against Manchester United; a score of first-team appearances, and then that swift promotion to England-international status. And, after England's 2-0 victory, there was a celebration drink – a pint of the "the usual" – orange and lemonade.

Graeme Souness is certainly a big fan of the Jones boy: "For a young player to come in and show so much composure in big games and so much overall class is incredible. I'm sure the Liverpool crowd who have watched him regularly wouldn't disagree with my opinion of him."

OLD TRAFFORD

WEMBLEY

⚽ TOP: IT'S A LONG WAY from Gresty Road to Wembley, but Rob made it in 1991-92, tussling with French star Manuel Amoros during the international.

⚽ ABOVE: THE JONES BOY collects his Barclays Young Eagle trophy, watched by his proud grand-dad, ex-Anfield Red, Bill.

BURROWS BLAST EARNS GROUNDSMAN £1,000!

AUGUST

Despite Ian Rush's absence, Liverpool left £1.2M signing, Mark Walters, on the bench when they kicked off against promoted Oldham Athletic at Anfield. Newcomers Dean Saunders and Mark Wright, together with 19-year-old Steve McManaman making his Football League bow, joined the old-stagers in the line-up but it was a situation which wasn't to last for very long, as injuries played havoc with team selection. Liverpool came from behind to win, 2-1, thanks to second-half goals from Houghton and Barnes.

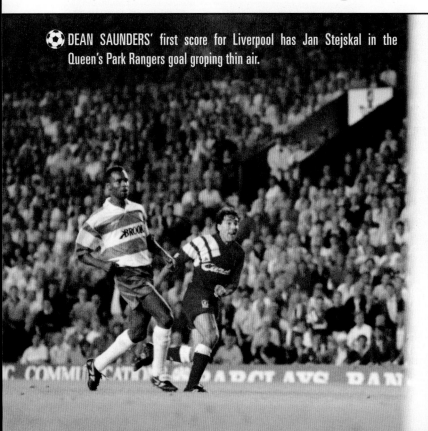

DEAN SAUNDERS' first score for Liverpool has Jan Stejskal in the Queen's Park Rangers goal groping thin air.

Trips to Manchester City and Luton followed, and those two matches yielded one point – a score-less draw at Luton. At Maine Road, McManaman opened his account but Saunders missed a late penalty to cost Liverpool a point, Dean's spot-kick shuddering the City bar. David White scored both of City's goals – ironically, his second came as the ball hit the underside of the bar and was ruled to have crossed the line. At Luton, Steve McMahon received marching orders after a foul and David Burrows saw a 30-yard thun-derbolt rebound from the angle of bar and post.

DEANO GETS OFF THE MARK

Two home games followed, and it was Dean Saunders' name being chanted by the Kop as he clinched victory over Queen's Park Rangers with the game's only goal. Graeme Souness had sent out one of the most inexperienced sides in recent Anfield history; Mark Wright joined a casualty list including Rush, Barnes, Whelan and Ablett. Nicky Tanner, Mike Marsh and Steve Harkness joined Steve McManaman as new faces in the line-up.

Saunders scored again when Liverpool met Everton – though David Burrows was probably the happiest Liverpool player, because he achieved an ambition after just one minute: to score in front of the Kop. His 20-yard drive earned Anfield's head groundsman the £1,000 Golden Goal prize! Saunders added a second after 15 minutes, and Ray Houghton made it 3-0 after just over an hour. Mike Newell's late goal was little consola-tion for Everton. However, Liverpool's injury list now included Glenn Hysen, Jimmy Carter, Jan Molby and Barry Venison, as well as Rush, Wright, Barnes and Whelan.

⚽ RAY HOUGHTON gets in front of Earl Barrett to score Liverpool's equaliser against Oldham.

⚽ KENNY DALGLISH back at Anfield – but as a spectator – for the kick-off day game against Oldham Athletic.

⚽RESULTS⚽

FOOTBALL LEAGUE
17 AUGUST

LIVERPOOL 2	OLDHAM ATHLETIC 1
Ray Houghton	Earl Barrett
John Barnes	

FOOTBALL LEAGUE
21 AUGUST

MANCHESTER CITY 2	LIVERPOOL 1
David White (2)	Steve McManaman

FOOTBALL LEAGUE
24 AUGUST

LUTON TOWN 0	LIVERPOOL 0

FOOTBALL LEAGUE
27 AUGUST

LIVERPOOL 1	QUEEN'S PARK
Dean Saunders	RANGERS 0

FOOTBALL LEAGUE
31 AUGUST

LIVERPOOL 3	EVERTON 1
David Burrows	Mike Newell
Dean Saunders	
Ray Houghton	

LEAGUE POSITION

	P	W	D	L	F	A	Pts	Position
Liverpool	5	3	1	1	7	4	10	Second

FOUR-GOAL RECORD
ON HIS EUROPEAN

Four League games, one UEFA Cup-tie and a Rumbelows-League Cup joust with Third Division Stoke City provided the programme for the month, starting with a trip to Notts County at Meadow Lane.

County had a made good start to the season, but though Tommy Johnson put them ahead just before half-time, Liverpool triumphed with late goals from substitute Ronny Rosenthal and an 89th minute Mark Walters penalty. Walters converted a hotly-disputed penalty in the next game too, as the Anfield Reds shared the spoils with Aston Villa, for whom Kevin Richardson struck early.

Then it was a switch to the European scene, with a first-leg UEFA Cup-tie against Finnish opposition at Anfield. Kuusysi Lahti were made to suffer, as Liverpool plundered half a dozen goals, while conceding only one. Dean Saunders scored four goals as, for the first time, he was paired with Ian Rush up front. Deano made the headlines, as he became the first Liverpool player to notch four in Europe, and Ray Houghton, in his 400th game, added the other two. They were two of eight players making European debuts; the others were: Mike Hooper, Gary Ablett, David Burrows,

⚽ RESULTS ⚽

FOOTBALL LEAGUE
7 SEPTEMBER

NOTTS COUNTY 1	LIVERPOOL 2
Tommy Johnson	Ronny Rosenthal
	Mark Walters (pen)

FOOTBALL LEAGUE
14 SEPTEMBER

LIVERPOOL 1	ASTON VILLA 1
Mark Walters (pen)	Kevin Richardson

FOOTBALL LEAGUE
21 SEPTEMBER

LEEDS UNITED 1	LIVERPOOL 0
Steve Hodge	

RUMBELOWS CUP
25 SEPTEMBER
(2ND ROUND, 1ST LEG)

LIVERPOOL 2	STOKE CITY 2
Ian Rush (2)	Ian Cranson
	Tony Kelly

FOOTBALL LEAGUE
28 SEPTEMBER

LIVERPOOL 1	SHEFFIELD WEDNESDAY 1
Ray Houghton	John Harkes

LEAGUE POSITION

	P	W	D	L	F	A	Pts	Position
Liverpool	9	4	3	2	11	8	15	Ninth

⚽ IAN RUSH scores one of his pair in the Rumbelows-League Cup match against Stoke City

DEBUT

Mike Marsh, Steve McMahon and Nicky Tanner, whose deflection gave the Finns their solitary goal.

LIVERPOOL LOSE THE WINNING HABIT

Leeds United at Elland Road were next on the agenda and Steve Nicol, making his 250th League appearance for Liverpool, insisted, "This will be our toughest test so far." The Rush-Saunders strike-force failed to click, so the goal by Steve Hodge, making his Leeds debut, clinched victory. Four days later, Third Division Stoke City came to Anfield, in the Rumbelows-League Cup, having managed only one draw from their last 26 visits. Ian Rush scored his first two goals of the season, but Stoke equalised twice, through Ian Cranson and Tony Kelly, to make things interesting for the second leg at Stoke.

The final match of the month saw Sheffield Wednesday's John Harkes score on his first visit to Anfield, to cancel Ray Houghton's earlier strike. Liverpool still had the chances to win, but it stayed 1-1.

⚽ RIGHT: RONNY ROSENTHAL is on his knees as the referee points to the penalty spot in the game against Aston Villa.

brucie
joins the exclusive
600 club

Bruce Grobbelaar has fielded the brickbats, as well as caught the bouquets, since he arrived at Liverpool. But despite all this, he has been the No.1 choice goalkeeper since joining the club from Vancouver Whitecaps in 1981. He has joined an exclusive club, with 600 appearances or more during his career.

⚽ BRUCE is always geeing up his team-mates.

Brucie is approaching Ian Callaghan, Ray Clemence, Emlyn Hughes, Tommy Smith and Alan Hansen, who all made more than 600 appearances in Liverpool's colours. Brucie took his career total past the 600 mark towards the end of season 1991-92.

CELEBRATION BLUES

He played his 400th League game for Liverpool against Crystal Palace, his 550th game overall for Liverpool at Peterborough, but both these matches were lost 1-0. Typically, he accepted some of the blame for Liverpool's biggest cup shock in 30

years. Amid speculation that Watford's David James would be joining Liverpool, Bruce admitted: "In my position, we're there to be shot at – literally. Any mistake is magnified, and this was a mistake, fair enough. But it came after a catalogue of mistakes by the team in that particular move. My error was just the final piece in the jigsaw." Bruce had already suffered, because he was dropped for the first time – on his 34th birthday – when Liverpool travelled to Manchester United. And the goal that brought Crystal Palace a League double over Liverpool was labelled a boob by Brucie.

BRILLIANT PERFORMANCES, TOO

In contrast, when Liverpool drew at West Ham, Bruce was superb, making many brilliant saves. After the draw at Southampton, Graeme Souness described his performance as "a classic demonstration of the art of last-line defending." The West Ham display earned him his first man-of-the-match bottle of champagne, and Bruce said the champers would be going on ice. "It's precious. Those awards don't come along too often, so I'm hanging on to it for now. If either of my daughters wants to break it open for a 21st birthday celebration, then the deed will be done." Since the girls were still only seven and three, it looks like staying on ice for a long time yet.

⚽ RIGHT: SIGN PLEASE ... and Brucie is happy to oblige.

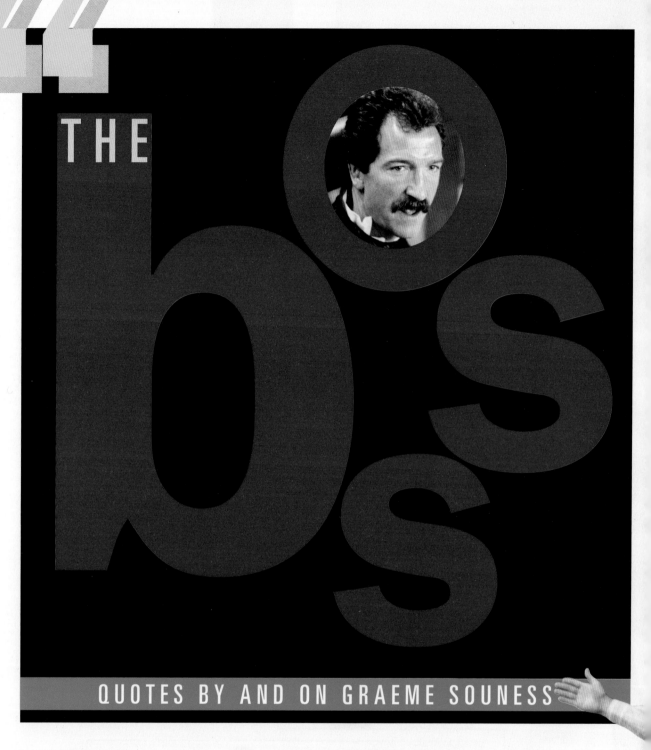

THE boss

QUOTES BY AND ON GRAEME SOUNESS

"The time to judge us is when my quality players are back in the side. Any team would miss John Barnes, Ronnie Whelan and Mark Wright."

GRAEME SOUNESS, in October 1991.
(When the three returned to action, Liverpool beat Aston Villa to reach the FA Cup semi-final.)

"Liverpool are in a healthier position than some people seem to think. When they can field their strongest line-up, they will be one hell of a team. All it needs now is a Souness of 10 years ago to provide great leadership on the park. The end of an era? Certainly not!"

FORMER LIVERPOOL CAPTAIN
Alan Hansen.

"Don't underestimate Liverpool. They're still one of the best sides in the First Division, and they won't be far away when the pots are handed out next May."

MANCHESTER CITY PLAYER-
MANAGER, Peter Reid.

⚽ "THE END OF AN ERA? Certainly not," says former skipper Alan Hansen.

"I couldn't believe it when I saw Liverpool being virtually written off. With the quality of players at Anfield you can never do that. Liverpool are still the side you have to beat, if you want to win trophies. They, along with Leeds, Manchester United, Everton and Arsenal, are capable of regularly winning European trophies and putting the rest of the Continent in the shade again."

LEEDS UNITED MIDFIELD STAR Gary McAllister.

"The style of football being played by an awful lot of top-flight clubs makes the job of winning the championship an enormous one. Their game is based on making life difficult for opponents, they try to prevent teams winning, rather than attempting to win themselves. Theirs is a 'let's not lose' attitude. These spoiling tactics are not new to me – I know I can combat them, but I won't change Liverpool's style to do so. The football at Anfield hasn't altered in the last 25 years. I'll try to maintain the style that has made Liverpool THE team to watch. The way Liverpool play is the right way."

GRAEME SOUNESS

⚽ GRAEME SOUNESS gets his point across.

17

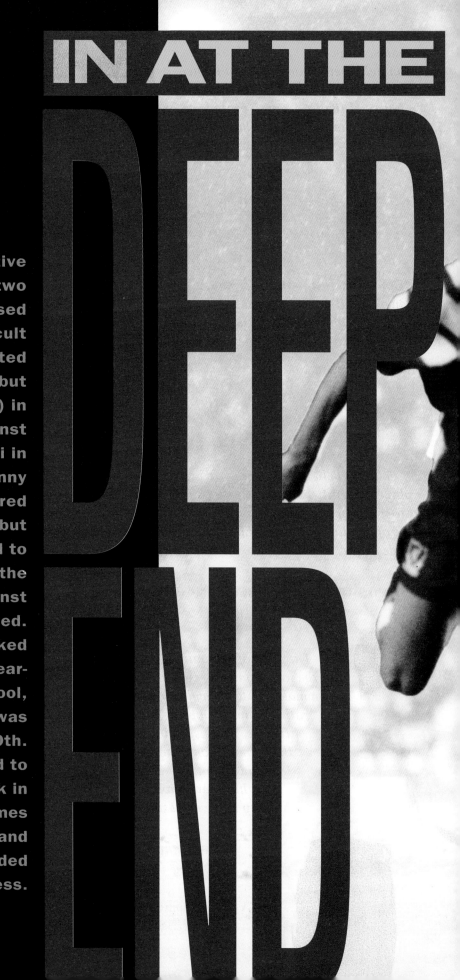

OCTOBER

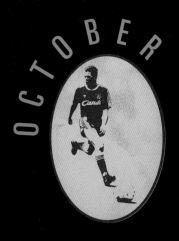

IN AT THE DEEP END

Five consecutive away games and two at home promised Liverpool a difficult month. It started with a 1-0 defeat (but 6-2 aggregate win) in the UEFA Cup against Kuuysysi Lahti in Finland. Ronny Rosenthal partnered Ian Rush up front, but Liverpool failed to score. Then came the test against Manchester United. Mike Hooper chalked up his 50th appearance for Liverpool, while Steve Nicol was making his 350th. Again, Rush failed to break his duck in twenty-plus games against United, and the game ended goal-less.

But the player who took the eye in this televised encounter was a young defender who had been signed from Crewe Alexandra only 72 hours earlier. Rob Jones, a £300,000 buy and grandson of former Liverpool player Bill Jones, was pitched straight in at the deep end, and though he made way for Mike Marsh, he acquitted himself well. Liverpool travelled to Stoke for their Rumbelows-League Cup replay, and goals from Steve McManaman, Dean Saunders and Mark Walters made it 3-1, before Wayne Biggins notched his second to complete the scoring.

RAY HOUGHTON acknowledges his match-winner against Coventry. Ogrizovic shows his disappointment.

TRANSFER TALK

At Chelsea, Steve McManaman put Liverpool ahead, but Vinny Jones and Andy Myers put the Blues 2-1 up, until Ian Rush drove in a shot which hit Paul Elliott and whizzed past 'keeper Kevin Hitchcock, to earn a point for Liverpool. Around this time there was talk of Liverpool signing 'keeper David James from Watford, though Bruce Grobbelaar produced some fine saves at Chelsea. Meantime, Jimmy Carter returned to London, signing for Arsenal.

For the UEFA Cup confrontation with Auxerre in Burgundy, Liverpool brought in 18-year-old Jamie Redknapp for his debut, but Auxerre won 2-0, Ferriri and Kovacs scoring. Home games followed in the League against Coventry and in the Rumbelows-League Cup against Port Vale. Jan Molby, in his first senior outing for close on six months, played a starring role against Coventry, Ray Houghton hitting the only goal of the game.

Port Vale shocked Liverpool, as they forged an early lead through Dutchman Robin van der Laan. Steve McManaman quickly equalised, and Ian Rush put Liverpool ahead, but Martin Foyle forced a replay.

IAN RUSH puts Liverpool 2-1 up against Port Vale in the rain.

RESULTS

FOOTBALL LEAGUE
6 OCTOBER

MANCHESTER UNITED 0	LIVERPOOL 0

RUMBELOWS CUP
9 OCTOBER
(2ND ROUND, 2ND LEG)

STOKE CITY 2	LIVERPOOL 3
Wayne Biggins	Steve McManaman
(2 – 1 pen)	Dean Saunders
	Mark Walters

FOOTBALL LEAGUE
19 OCTOBER

CHELSEA 2	LIVERPOOL 2
Vinny Jones	Steve McManaman
Andrew Myers	Paul Elliott
	(own goal)

FOOTBALL LEAGUE
26 OCTOBER

LIVERPOOL 1	COVENTRY CITY 0
Ray Houghton	

RUMBELOWS CUP
29 OCTOBER (3RD ROUND)

LIVERPOOL 2	PORT VALE 2
Steve McManaman	Robin Van der Laan
Ian Rush	Martin Foyle

LEAGUE POSITION

	P	W	D	L	F	A	Pts	Position
Liverpool	12	5	5	2	14	10	20	Eighth

NOVEMBER

TOPS IN EUROPE

Liverpool's cup performances this month overshadowed their First Division exploits. After the home game against Crystal Palace, it was Steve Coppell who was smiling. Graeme Souness's verdict was terse: "I feel as if we've been mugged." Glenn Hysen had given his side a first-half lead, but Liverpool's luck ran out soon after the break as Marco Gabbiadini equalised and Geoff Thomas wrapped up the points with a header. It was Palace's first win at Anfield.

THE CUP THAT CHEERS

Liverpool had to bounce back when they entertained Auxerre trying to wipe out the 2-0 first leg deficit in the UEFA Cup. After four minutes, Jan Molby converted a penalty to put Liverpool on their way. After half an hour, Mike Marsh levelled the aggregate with his first goal for the club, and seven minutes from time, Liverpool made sure when Mark Walters struck their third goal.

In the televised game at West Ham on the Sunday, the man-of-the-match vote went to 'keeper Bruce Grobbelaar, for three fine saves in a no-score draw. The Rumbelows-League Cup replay at Vale Park was next, and Liverpool stylishly won through, 4-1. Steve McManaman opened the scoring, Martin Foyle replied almost immediately, before Mark Walters, Ray Houghton, and Dean Saunders completed the scoring.

Wimbledon have always presented Liverpool with problems, and

⚽ JAN MOLBY gets some pre-Christmas cheer, picking up a man-of-the-match award.

in their next League match, it was no exception. A forgettable 0-0 draw resulted. Liverpool resumed the UEFA Cup trail with a trip to Austria for their first-leg tie against Swarovski Tirol. Dean Saunders hit two goals, while the Liverpool defence stood firm, so the journey home was a happy one.

Norwich City came to Anfield for the final match of the month, and the result was a 2-1 Liverpool victory. After three minutes, Jan Molby struck what many people rated the goal

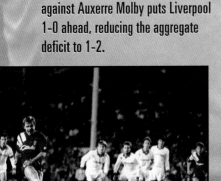

⚽ JAN MOLBY...his goal against Norwich was "the best that's ever been struck against me", said Canaries 'keeper Bryan Gunn.

⚽ FOUR MINUTES into the UEFA Cup tie against Auxerre Molby puts Liverpool 1-0 ahead, reducing the aggregate deficit to 1-2.

of the season; Ian Butterworth blocked Gary Ablett's free-kick, and the ball fell for Liverpool's great Dane to take aim and fire; it flew into the top right-hand corner, leaving 'keeper Bryan Gunn to gasp: "That's the best goal that's ever been struck against me." Gunn blocked another Molby effort which had deflected off Dean Saunders, but Ray Houghton followed up to score the second goal.

⚽ RESULTS ⚽

FOOTBALL LEAGUE
2 NOVEMBER

LIVERPOOL 1	CRYSTAL PALACE 2
Glenn Hysen	Marco Gabbiadini
	Geoff Thomas

FOOTBALL LEAGUE
17 NOVEMBER

WEST HAM UNITED 0	LIVERPOOL 0

RUMBELOWS CUP
20 NOVEMBER
(3RD ROUND, REPLAY)

PORT VALE 1	LIVERPOOL 4
Martin Foyle	Steve McManaman
	Mark Walters
	Ray Houghton
	Dean Saunders

FOOTBALL LEAGUE
23 NOVEMBER

WIMBLEDON 0	LIVERPOOL 0

FOOTBALL LEAGUE
30 NOVEMBER

LIVERPOOL 2	NORWICH CITY 1
Jan Molby	Darren Beckford
Ray Houghton	

LEAGUE POSITION

	P	W	D	L	F	A	Pts	Position
Liverpool	16	6	7	3	17	13	25	Ninth

⚽ MARK WALTERS slides in the the match-winner late in the game with Auxerre.

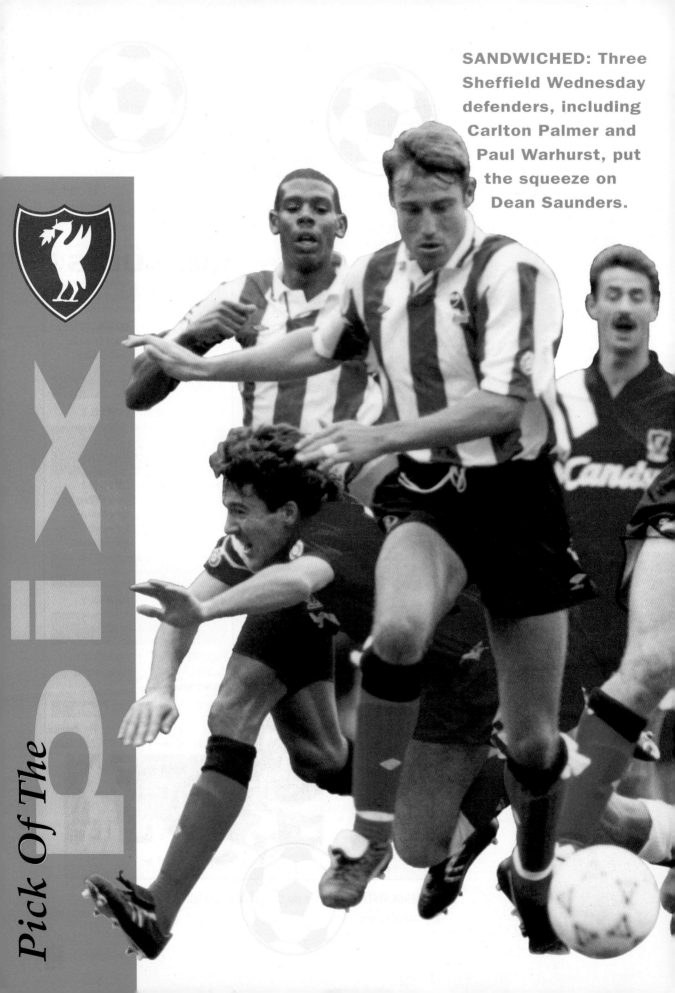

SANDWICHED: Three Sheffield Wednesday defenders, including Carlton Palmer and Paul Warhurst, put the squeeze on Dean Saunders.

Pick Of The PIX

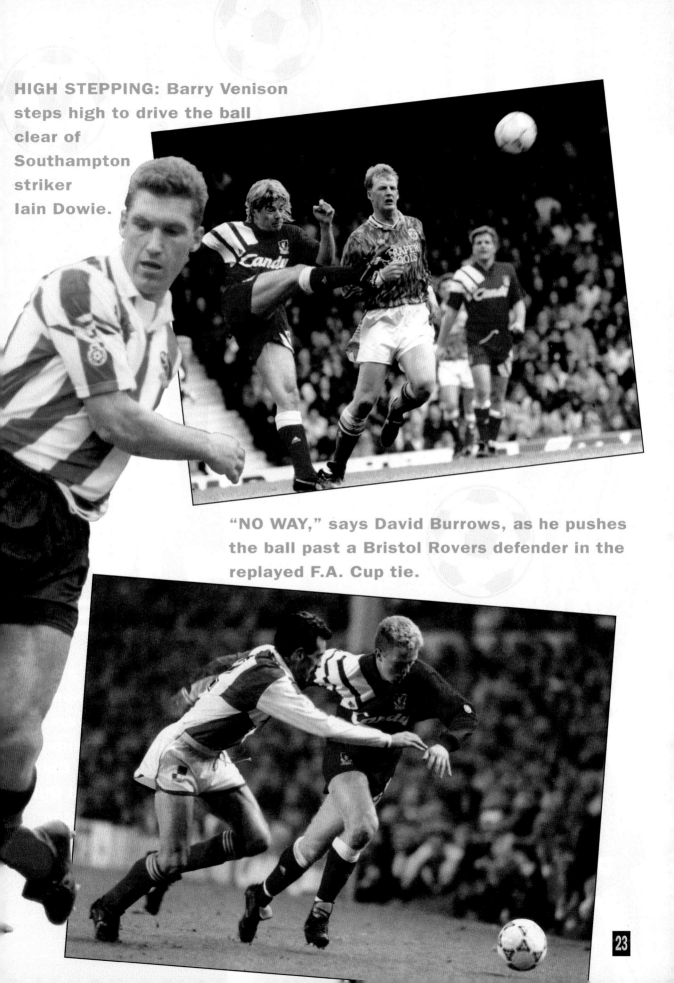

HIGH STEPPING: Barry Venison steps high to drive the ball clear of Southampton striker Iain Dowie.

"NO WAY," says David Burrows, as he pushes the ball past a Bristol Rovers defender in the replayed F.A. Cup tie.

A FAMILY AFFAIR

ADDS UP TO 2,400 -PLUS

PHIL THOMPSON... Like Ron Yeats, he skippered Liverpool, and together they totalled more than 900 appearances through 22 seasons.

Liverpool have a great reputation for keeping jobs for ex-players, on the backroom side: "in the family". Bob Paisley followed Bill Shankly, Joe Fagan succeeded Bob, Kenny Dalglish came next, and now there's Graeme Souness as manager.

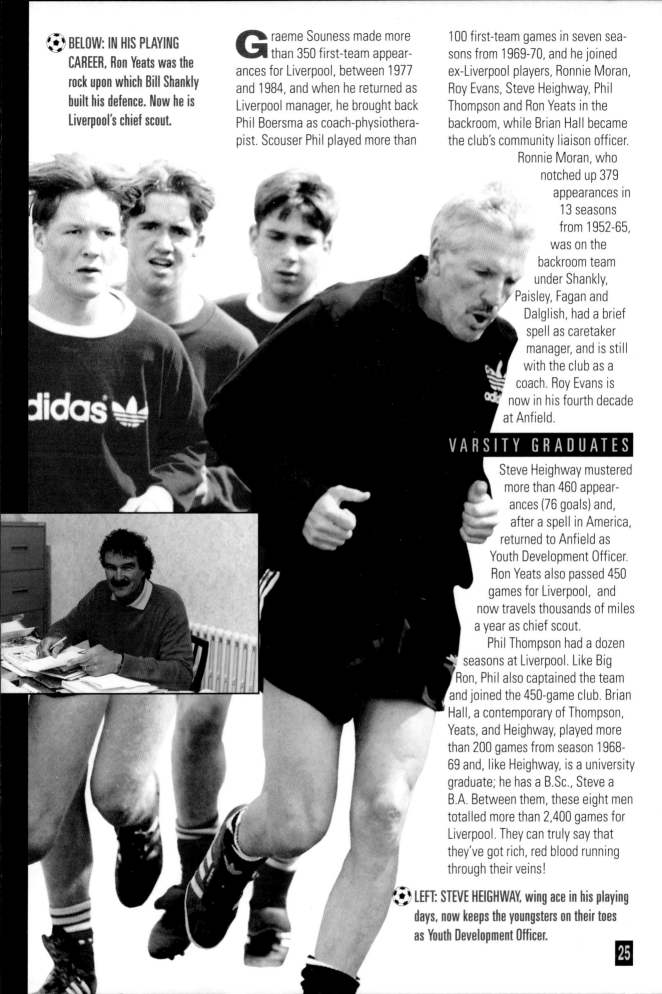

Graeme Souness made more than 350 first-team appearances for Liverpool, between 1977 and 1984, and when he returned as Liverpool manager, he brought back Phil Boersma as coach-physiotherapist. Scouser Phil played more than 100 first-team games in seven seasons from 1969-70, and he joined ex-Liverpool players, Ronnie Moran, Roy Evans, Steve Heighway, Phil Thompson and Ron Yeats in the backroom, while Brian Hall became the club's community liaison officer.

Ronnie Moran, who notched up 379 appearances in 13 seasons from 1952-65, was on the backroom team under Shankly, Paisley, Fagan and Dalglish, had a brief spell as caretaker manager, and is still with the club as a coach. Roy Evans is now in his fourth decade at Anfield.

VARSITY GRADUATES

Steve Heighway mustered more than 460 appearances (76 goals) and, after a spell in America, returned to Anfield as Youth Development Officer. Ron Yeats also passed 450 games for Liverpool, and now travels thousands of miles a year as chief scout.

Phil Thompson had a dozen seasons at Liverpool. Like Big Ron, Phil also captained the team and joined the 450-game club. Brian Hall, a contemporary of Thompson, Yeats, and Heighway, played more than 200 games from season 1968-69 and, like Heighway, is a university graduate; he has a B.Sc., Steve a B.A. Between them, these eight men totalled more than 2,400 games for Liverpool. They can truly say that they've got rich, red blood running through their veins!

THE DERBY DAY
DUELS

Liverpool collected four points from their annual derby-game duels with Everton; three points at Anfield and a some-what fortunate point in the Goodison Park return.

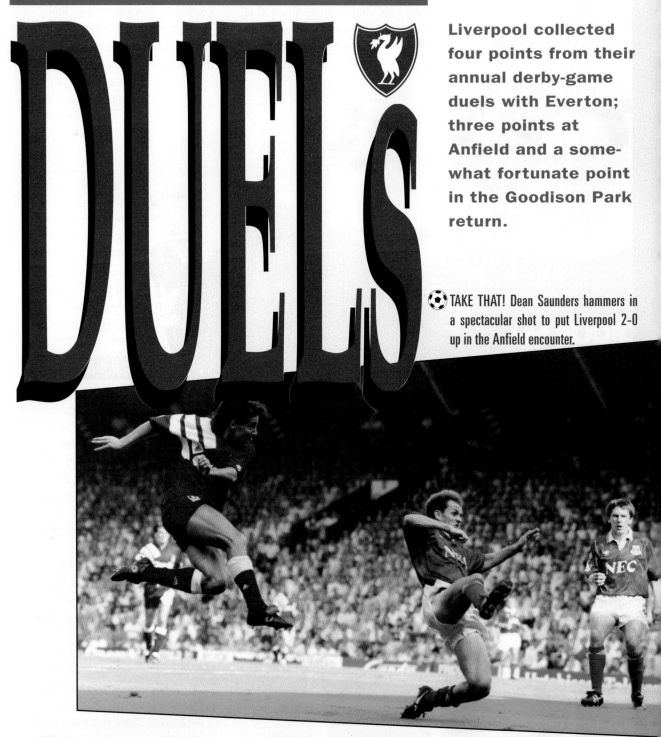

⚽ TAKE THAT! Dean Saunders hammers in a spectacular shot to put Liverpool 2-0 up in the Anfield encounter.

The 145th Merseyside derby produced a 54th triumph for Liverpool, despite the absence of Ian Rush, John Barnes and Mark Wright.

David Burrows' goal was notable, as it was the third-fastest derby-game goal of all time. For many

years a goal scored by Dixie Dean after 32 seconds held the record; then came Kenny Dalglish, with a 20-second goal at Goodison; and now David Burrows, with a goal after 48 seconds, as he struck from the edge of the penalty area.

Then, Dean Saunders struck a spectacular effort – it was a sizzling goal on his derby-game debut – and Ray Houghton made it 3-0 from a Burrows pass, before Mike Newell scored a consolation goal for

ACTION-MAN Ray Houghton, one of Liverpool's marksmen in the Anfield Derby Duel.

Everton, thanks to a pass from former Liverpool idol Peter Beardsley who, otherwise, had an unhappy afternoon against his old team-mates.

A POINT AT GOODISON

In the Goodison return, Liverpool took the lead again, thanks to a first-ever goal from defender Nicky Tanner in the opening half. A right-wing corner from Dean Saunders went into the crowded penalty area, new-boy Michael Thomas added a touch, and Tanner stabbed the ball over the line. Mark Ward scrambled the ball away, but his claim that it hadn't crossed the line cut no ice with referee Vic Callow.

It was left to Everton's £1.5M signing, Mo Johnston, to cure Everton's blues as he hit the equaliser in a game which was labelled "a tremendous advert for British Soccer." Johnston cashed in on the absence of Mark Wright, who suffered a "dead leg" and didn't resume after half-time. As at Anfield, Peter Beardsley contributed to Everton's goal; a perfect header released Matthew Jackson, and when the right back tried to hammer home a shot, the ball flew across the face of goal and the unmarked Johnston turned it into the net.

NEVILLE SOUTHALL rushes out of his area to kick the ball clear from the oncoming Mike Marsh.

RUMBELOWS

RED Faces

Liverpool played eight matches in December, but one result sent shock waves throughout football.

Their fourth round tie of the Rumbelows-League Cup sent the Anfield Reds to Peterborough United, and the Posh handed Liverpool their most humiliating cup defeat since being knocked out of the FA Cup by minnows Worcester City in 1959; Gary Kimble's 19th minute strike was enough.

NICKY TANNER'S first goal for Liverpool came against the rivals from across Stanley Park.

JAN MOLBY'S free kick causes anguish for Mark Crossley in the Nottingham Forest goal, as the ball crosses the line.

28

Bruce Grobbelaar, blamed for the Peterborough goal, defied Southampton at the Dell in the next match, while 18-year-old Jamie Redknapp, on his First Division bow, weighed in with a goal which earned a point.

ANOTHER HAT-TRICK

The next game brought UEFA Cup opponents, Swarovski Tirol, to Anfield, and Liverpool added four goals to their 2-0 first leg lead. Man of the match, Dean Saunders, scored another European hat-trick.

Nottingham Forest came to Anfield three days later, and left on the wrong end of a 2-0 scoreline, Steve McMahon scoring his first League goal for two seasons and Jan Molby notching the other. The talk over this weekend however, revolved around Liverpool's £1.5M new arrival, Michael Thomas, and Steve McMahon, who was about to depart. And so to White Hart Lane, with McMahon still claiming the No.11 shirt, and Thomas having to settle for No.12, though Thomas did replace Molby and Marsh went on for McMahon. Dean Saunders and Houghton sealed a 2-1 win.

A week later, Manchester City visited, and David White, as he had done at Maine Road, grabbed both goals, but Liverpool also scored twice. Deano gave Liverpool an early lead, White struck twice, but substitute Mike Marsh laid on Steve Nicol's equaliser. Steve McMahon, taken off during the game, joined City soon afterwards.

FIRST EVER GOAL

After a scoreless draw at Loftus Road with Queen's Park Rangers, Liverpool then travelled to Goodison Park for the second meeting with Everton. It ended in a 1-1 draw, £1.5M signing Mo Johnston cancelling out Nicky Tanner's first goal for Liverpool. Mark Wright went off injured at half-time and his absence gave former Liverpool ace Peter Beardsley the space to play a part in Johnston's equaliser.

⚽ **MICHAEL THOMAS** made a quick return to London, coming on to replace Molby at Tottenham Hotspur.

JANUARY

BARNES BACK with THREE-GOAL COP

Liverpool opened 1992 with a New Year's Day home match against Sheffield United. Dave Bassett's strugglers got away to a flier, scoring their first goal at Anfield in almost 25 years, Brian Deane netting, and held on until the second half when substitute Steve McManaman set up Ray Houghton's equaliser. Then, 10 minutes from time, Dean Saunders hit the winner – in off a post. Blades 'keeper Simon Tracey claimed, "It was a mis-hit ... if he'd hit it straight, I might have got it."

⚽ RESULTS ⚽

FOOTBALL LEAGUE 1 JANUARY

LIVERPOOL 2	SHEFFIELD UNITED 1
Ray Houghton	Brian Deane
Dean Saunders	

FOOTBALL LEAGUE 11 JANUARY

LIVERPOOL 2	LUTON TOWN 1
Steve McManaman	Nicky Tanner
Dean Saunders	(own goal)

FOOTBALL LEAGUE 18 JANUARY

OLDHAM ATHLETIC 2	LIVERPOOL 3
Neil Adams	Steve McManaman
Paul Bernard	Dean Saunders
	Michael Thomas

FOOTBALL LEAGUE 29 JANUARY

LIVERPOOL 2	ARSENAL 0
Jan Molby (penalty)	
Ray Houghton	

LEAGUE POSITION

	P	W	D	L	F	A	Pts	Position
Liverpool	26	12	11	3	34	22	47	Ninth

BACK TO CREWE

Rob Jones returned to the team where he started the season, as Liverpool travelled to Crewe for the third round of the FA Cup; but the star of the show turned out to be John Barnes, back in action after an absence of 32 matches. He scored a hat-trick, as Liverpool won 4-0. After Steve McManaman's opener, John reacted swiftly to deflect a Dean Saunders shot home; 90 seconds later came a right-foot volley after a one-two with Steve McManaman; and in the last minute, a penalty goal.

Liverpool then entertained relegation-haunted Luton Town. And for Nicky Tanner, it was a game to remember for the wrong reason; he scored an own goal from a nightmare back-pass, and Luton held on until, in the 85th minute, Mark Wright met a Ray Houghton cross, and Steve McManaman scrambled the ball home. In injury time, John Barnes's inch-perfect cross was tucked away at the near post by Dean Saunders.

DOUBLE DELIGHT

A trip to Oldham followed, with Liverpool looking for a double, after their 2-1 win on kick-off day. They managed it, 3-2, though Oldham never quit. After Dean Saunders and

BLAST

Steve McManaman scored, £1.5M new-boy Michael Thomas notched his first goal for the club. The next match brought Michael's former club, Arsenal, to Anfield. Fortune favoured Liverpool; after Arsenal had done everything but score, the Anfield Reds gained a penalty, and Jan Molby (who else?) made no mistake; then Ray Houghton scored a beauty, to complete a 2-0 victory.

⚽ BELOW: MICHAEL THOMAS's first goal for Liverpool proved the winner against Oldham.

⚽ ABOVE: STEVE MCMANAMAN has split the Crewe defence in more ways than one as he scores the opening goal in the FA Cup tie at Gresty Road.

⚽ ABOVE: JAN MOLBY is about to put Liverpool 1-0 up from the penalty spot in the League encounter against Arsenal.

Quiz?

QUESTIONS

1 Rob Jones indulges in aerial ballet – but can you name Liverpool's opposition? PICTURE A

2 Which goalkeeper saved a penalty against Liverpool in an FA Cup final, for which team and in which year?

3 Look at the jersey ... now name the wearer. PICTURE B

4 It's a red card, though not for Mark Walters. Can you name the team whose player is being sent off? PICTURE C

5 Which lower-division club suffered its heaviest-ever FA Cup defeat at the hands of Liverpool at the start of the 1990s?

6 Which number did Graeme Souness normally wear during his years as a first-team regular at Anfield?

A

B

C

7 John Barnes and Kenny Jackett shared the same honour at Watford. What was it?

8 This player hit his first hat-trick for Liverpool against Notts County in 1982. What is his name?

9 Mark Walters is easy ... but can you name the No. 2? PICTURE D

10 Who is the Liverpool player and the referee getting a drink? PICTURE E

11 Which player headed the goal that took the FA Cup to Anfield for the first time?

12 Which player is tangling with Dean Saunders and can you name the two First Division clubs he played for in 1991/92? PICTURE F

F

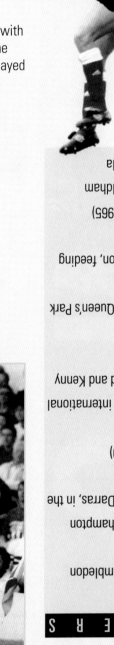

E

D

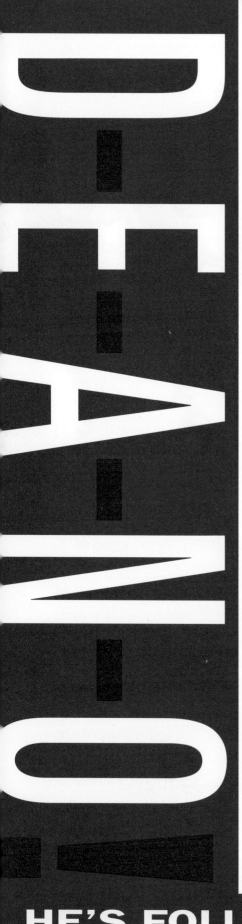

D·E·A·N·O!

HE'S FOLLOWED IN DAD'S FOOTSTEPS

In 1985, Swansea City gave Dean Saunders a free transfer. In July 1991, Liverpool paid Derby County a British record fee of £2.9M to land Deano from under the noses of Everton and Nottingham Forest. When he left Derby, manager Arthur Cox told Dean: "Don't let me down; I expect you to score 20 goals a season."

Deano passed that target in March, 1992, and became a club-record marksman in Europe. It was a long road from Swansea, via Brighton, Oxford United and Derby, to Liverpool, for whom Dean's father, Roy, had played almost 150 games in the 1950's. Dad had helped Dean from his schooldays: "He couldn't coach me to score goals, but he would tell me how to move into the right positions."

AN ALL-ROUNDER

"I was an all-rounder – fortunate enough to be good at cricket, golf, rugby, tennis and snooker. With the right coaching, I might have had a go at making the grade as a cricketer." And the most important rule Dad instilled into Deano? – "The need to make a contribution in other areas of the field – if you're an out-and-out striker, you must be hitting the net all the time; otherwise you're no use to anyone. Throughout my career I've tried to keep involved in everything; when the goals have dried up, I've had the satisfaction of knowing I've helped the team in other ways."

Arthur Cox drummed that philosophy into Deano, too. "Before I left, he emphasised I'd have to keep making an overall contribution, if I were to be successful. I've learned something from all my managers, but Arthur was probably the most influential."

TOTALLY CONVINCED

Maurice Evans signed Deano for Oxford for £55,000, and Oxford sold him for £1M. Maurice says: "I saw Dean playing in one game – at West Brom – and though he missed three or four chances, I was totally convinced he would score goals." Deano has shown this, especially in European action; but there's another record he doesn't want: he has been relegated with each of his four previous clubs.

⚽ AFTER HIS UEFA Cup four-timer against Finns Kuusysi Lahti, Deano hit a hat-trick against Swarovski Tirol of Austria. Here's one of them.

DEAN SAUNDERS leaves Chelsea's Ken Monkou trailing in his wake.

BELOW RIGHT: International team-mates, and now club-mates, Dean with Ian

35

'BIG HEADS'

BUT CUP EXPLOITS

spare blushes

⚽ STEVE McMANAMAN'S winning goal in the FA Cup replay against Ipswich makes Bruce Grobbelaar a happy man!

February began badly as Chelsea enjoyed a first League win at Anfield for 57 years. Ronny Rosenthal equalised Vinny Jones' opener, but Dennis Wise, who saw Bruce Grobbelaar brilliantly save his earlier penalty, got the winner. Graeme Souness observed: "That's the most disappointing home performance since I came here."

Bristol Rovers away in the FA Cup was also difficult. Only five minutes after Dean Saunders had given Liverpool a first-half lead, Rovers had a penalty appeal rejected. Another Saunders - Carl - equalised after an hour, to earn the men from Bath a replay. A trip to Coventry followed and Grobbelaar's saves earned Liverpool a point.

BIRTHDAY BOY

Carl Saunders put Bristol Rovers ahead in the Cup replay at Anfield, but Steve McManaman, celebrating his 20th birthday, turned the game. He cut in from the right and drove in the equaliser, then he went almost the length of the pitch, put Dean Saunders away on the left, and saw Deano clip the winner. Ian Rush came on for his first appearance after two knee operations.

Next came Ipswich Town away in the fifth round. Former Liverpool man John Wark was at the heart of the Ipswich defence and, as well as keeping Dean Saunders and Ian Rush quiet, he almost scored, hitting the Liverpool crossbar with a header. Liverpool's Hungarian import, Istvan Kozma, came on to help his side hold out for a 0-0 draw. Liverpool travelled to East Anglia again, for the League game against Norwich City at Carrow Road, but fell to a 3-0 defeat, their biggest defeat of the season.

⚽ STOP-ACTION SEQUENCE as Steve McManaman scores Liverpool's FA Cup-winner against Ipswich Town at Anfield.

⚽RESULTS⚽

FOOTBALL LEAGUE 1 FEBRUARY	
LIVERPOOL 1	CHELSEA 2
Ronny Rosenthal	Vinny Jones
	Dennis Wise

FOOTBALL LEAGUE 8 FEBRUARY	
COVENTRY CITY 0	LIVERPOOL 0

FOOTBALL LEAGUE 22 FEBRUARY	
NORWICH CITY 3	LIVERPOOL 0
Colin Woodthorpe	
Robert Fleck (2)	

FOOTBALL LEAGUE 29 FEBRUARY	
LIVERPOOL 0	SOUTHAMPTON 0

LEAGUE POSITION							
Liverpool	P	W	D	L	F	A	Pts	Position
	30	12	13	5	35	27	49	Fifth

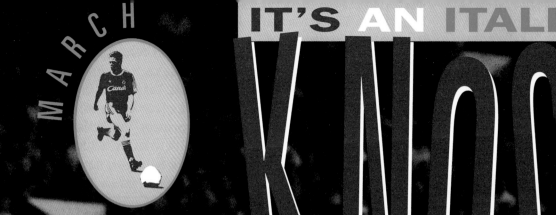

IT'S AN ITALIAN
KNOCK

March saw Liverpool's UEFA Cup hopes demolished, as Genoa became only the third club to win both legs against them in European competition; but if that defeat spelled a knock-out blow in one arena, Liverpool still managed to come up smiling, as they disposed of Aston Villa in the FA Cup sixth round.

⚽ RAY HOUGHTON is all smiles as he collects the player of the year award from the Shrewsbury branch of Liverpool Supporters Club.

Down 2-0 after the away leg of the UEFA Cup, Liverpool showed resilience by staging a comeback in the domestic cup competition as they pitched John Barnes, Ronnie Whelan and Michael Thomas into the action after long injury lay-offs; the gamble paid off, as Thomas scored the only goal.

In the League, Liverpool lost to an Eric Young goal at Selhurst Park, allowing Crystal Palace to achieve their first-ever double over the Anfield Reds. West Ham, though, suffered as Liverpool scored the only goal of the game at Anfield, with Dean Saunders claiming his 21st of the season. After being stuck on 20 in his last four seasons elsewhere, Deano vowed: "Now I'll aim towards 30." Saunders then notched a pair in the 2-1 win over Tottenham. The Londoners were unlucky losers at Anfield, just as Liverpool were against Genoa, four days later.

Ian Rush's goal sandwiched between a pair from Carlos Aguilera, was the sole reward for incessant pressure. After the disappointment of the UEFA Cup exit, Liverpool went to Sheffield United looking for a League boost. Mark Wright, Dean Saunders, John Barnes and Nicky Tanner were missing, though Ronnie Whelan, Michael Thomas and Ray Houghton played, but it was a poor display; manager Graeme Souness described Brian Deane's first goal as "like something out of a comic strip."

The month ended brightly as Notts. County left Anfield 4-0 losers. More importantly, Liverpool ended March with the squad all fully fit and available, except for the suspended Dean Saunders.

⚽ **THE ANGUISH** shows on Gary Mabbutt's face as Deano equalises against Spurs.

⚽ RESULTS ⚽

FOOTBALL LEAGUE 11 MARCH	
LIVERPOOL 1	**WEST HAM UNITED 0**
Dean Saunders	

FOOTBALL LEAGUE 14 MARCH	
CRYSTAL PALACE 1	**LIVERPOOL 0**
Eric Young	

FOOTBALL LEAGUE 21 MARCH	
LIVERPOOL 2	**TOTTENHAM HOTSPUR 1**
Dean Saunders (2)	Paul Stewart

FOOTBALL LEAGUE 28 MARCH	
SHEFFIELD UNITED 2	**LIVERPOOL 0**
Brian Deane (2)	

FOOTBALL LEAGUE 31 MARCH	
LIVERPOOL 4	**NOTTS COUNTY 0**
Michael Thomas	
Steve McManaman	
Ian Rush	
Barry Venison	

LEAGUE POSITION

	P	W	D	L	F	A	Pts	Position
Liverpool	35	15	13	7	42	31	58	Fourth

The right man for the job

He swiftly learned on his arrival at Anfield that "there are no favourites here. Everybody is treated the same, regardless of name or reputation." By joining Liverpool, Mark fulfilled his Dad's ambition; Alan Wright is Liverpool-born, and an Anfield Reds fan. With relatives still on Merseyside, Mark soon felt at home, on and off the field.

'ANSWER TO ME!'

His first match as captain was at The Dell, against former club Southampton, and he received a telegram from his boss at Derby County, Arthur Cox. It read: "Better players than you have been captain of Liverpool. It is now your problem to live up to your predecessors' achievements. If you don't, you'll have to answer to me." Mark was captain under Cox at Derby and he acknowledged: "He knows what makes me tick, he knows how much I hate losing. But I've come here to win prizes, not to be a failure. I never won here with Southampton or Derby. For the first time, I feel I'm on the right side."

KAISER FRANZ

Mark has had many influences on his career: "Alan Ball at Southampton had everything as a captain; he led by example, but also read the game superbly. Steve Williams was a big help to me, too." Oddly enough, his career has run parallel with that of Dean Saunders – both played for Oxford United and Derby County. While Deano has been a regular for Wales, Mark has stayed in the England spotlight. His favourite player almost redefined the art of defending: "Franz Beckenbauer, a defender who could score goals and play almost anywhere, despite the quality of opposition." Some judges say there is a lot of Franz in Mark's play.

MARK WRIGHT jumps high to clear from Jason Dozzell in the FA Cup replay with Ipswich.

Mark Wright's first season at Anfield had many challenges: to follow former greats such as Ron Yeats and Alan Hansen at the heart of the defence; an injury early on put Mark out for three months; there was his £2.2M transfer; and the responsibility of captaincy.

MARK FOLLOWS "THE BOSS"

WALTERS TUSSLES with Notts County defender Alan Paris.

Mark Walters (£1.2M) and Michael Thomas (£1.5M) were big-money signings by manager Graeme Souness as he fortified his ageing and injury-hit squad.

THREE LEAGUE TITLES

Souness had signed Mark Walters for Glasgow Rangers, and when the boss returned to Anfield, Mark rejoined him. The winger commented: "I matured as a player and a person under Graeme at Ibrox. Enough, in fact, for him to consider me capable of being a Liverpool player. I'd had things too easy at Villa. Graeme taught me about preparing for matches, showed me the value of the right lifestyle; I was drinking pop, not eating the right food to boost my energy. And on the field the manager made me a more intelligent player." Mark helped Rangers to win three consecutive League titles, though he admitted it was harder to settle in at Anfield, "I'd forgotten the high level of technical ability needed to compete in the First Division."

If Liverpool ever need a penalty-taker to follow Jan Molby, Mark's their man. "I always fancy my chances of scoring. I'm not scared of missing; nerves don't bother me. I have videos which show both Maradona and Pele failing from the spot, so there's always an excuse for me!"

Walters remembers his early days as a Villa fan when a match lasted no more than 10 minutes, for him. Aged seven, Mark could not afford admission, so he only got in to see the end of their games, once the gates had been opened to let the early leavers depart.

MICHAEL SEES THE WHEEL TURN

FULL CIRCLE

⚽ **SOON AFTER** his £1.5M transfer from Arsenal, Michael Thomas was in action against Manchester City.

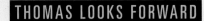

THOMAS LOOKS FORWARD

Michael Thomas supported Spurs as a boy, considered signing for Chelsea, but finally joined the Gunners. Signing for Liverpool meant the wheel of soccer fortune was turning full circle because, in May 1989, Michael scored the last-second goal that won Arsenal the championship at Anfield. After signing, he said: "That's in the past; I think only Liverpool thoughts now." To prove it he scored a brilliant first goal in the FA Cup win over Sunderland

43

Bob
bows out

⚽ BOB PAISLEY and Graeme Souness with the European Cup.

Shortly before Liverpool celebrated their centenary, in March, 1992, Bob Paisley despatched a letter to Anfield that ended an era. It read: "Owing to ill-health, I can no longer maintain my place as an active member of the board of Liverpool FC. I have served the club for over 50 years, and to be elected to the board was the final accolade. I thank all my fellow board-members for the pleasure it has been to work with them."

⚽ BOB PAISLEY, the trainer, together with the Liverpool team of the early 1960s. How many can you name?

BOB DOES IT ALL

On May 8, 1939, Bob Paisley arrived at Anfield as a young hopeful from famous Amateurs, Bishop Auckland. He stayed as player, trainer, coach, physiotherapist, assistant manager, manager and director. During his time as Liverpool's manager between 1974 and 1983, the club collected six First Division titles, three European Cups, three Milk Cups, the UEFA Cup, and Bob was named Manager of the Year six times.

The Nottingham Forest manager Brian Clough said about the man who always remained modest, even humble, despite all his success: "Bob was a genius. I hope I survive in the game as long as he did."

Bob knew football inside-out, but would have been happy to remain in the background at Liverpool. As he said at the time he took over: "I hope the team will do the talking for me." And indeed, it did.

THE ANFIELD STYLE

He inherited the backroom team Bill Shankly had built around himself at Anfield, so in Joe Fagan and Ronnie Moran he knew he had trusted lieutenants. Joe succeeded Bob as manager, and he recalled: "People said I should have been afraid to follow Bob, in view of the trophies he won. I never was, because nobody could have followed him."

Bob Paisley was made a Freeman of the City, went to Buckingham Palace to meet the Queen, and on his retirement from football the club made him a life vice-president. How

⚽ BOB PAISLEY, the manager, standing by a picture of Bob Paisley, the schoolboy footballer.

did he see himself, during his time at Anfield? Bob replied, "I became part of the furniture.". And there will always be a part of Bob Paisley at Liverpool Football Club.

IT'S THE SAUNDERS-BARNES SHOW:
hat-trick heroes

John Barnes and Dean Saunders had their share of problems during 1991-92. The England wing ace was sidelined through injury too often for his liking, while the Welsh international initially found League goals harder to come by than they were in European competition. But both men had their moments of glory, because each became a hat-trick hero – Deano twice over.

In the UEFA Cup, he scored four goals against the Finns of Kuusysi Lahti at Anfield, then he followed up by hitting a brace against Swarovski Tirol in the away leg and hammering a hat-trick against the Austrians in the Anfield return. The four-timer was the first for Liverpool in European competition.

John Barnes? He had missed 32 matches when he came back for the third-round FA Cup-tie against Crewe Alexandra at Gresty Road, and he made Rob Jones's old team-mates suffer as he scored a hat-trick.

Here we feature some of the goals that made Deano and John headliners.

⚽ DEAN SAUNDERS loves European football. He wheels away after making the score 4-1 against Kuusysi Lahti in the UEFA Cup first round.

⚽ TWO ROUNDS LATER, it is the Swarovski Tirol 'keeper who was on the receiving end of a Saunders hat-trick.

⚽ JOHN BARNES scores his second goal against Crewe Alexandra in the FA Cup third round ...

⚽ .. AND IN THE LAST MINUTE, he is bundled over for a penalty, which he converted in the 4-0 win.

He's not quite Stevie Wonder yet, but...

A bonus for Liverpool from the injury-plagued 1991-92 season was that some of the youngsters came into the first team and did a good job. Nicky Tanner – though he was an experienced reserve-team player – blocked the way to goal when he was pitched into the senior side at centre-back. Then there was Mike Marsh, whose sterling displays earned him a new three and a half year deal, less than a year after he had signed his current contract. "The boss made the offer, and I had no hesitation in agreeing," said a delighted Mike.

⚽ STEVE McMANAMAN takes on Oldham's Earl Barrett on his debut in August 1991.

FIRST SILVERWARE

And what about Steve McManaman, who made an impact in the first match of season 1991-92, against Oldham Athletic at Anfield? He claimed the Barclays Young Eagle award for August and so, at the age of 19, collected his first piece of silverware. But Steve's feet were kept firmly on the ground. As team-coach Phil Thompson explained: "Youngsters here are not encouraged to believe their own publicity; there was no fanfare of trumpets at Anfield. He came here at the age of 14 from Liverpool Schoolboys and trained two evenings a week."

"He suffered the wrath of coaches over the years, but seemed to come to terms with his teachings. It helps that he's a Merseysider; others have travelled the same road before him: Tommy Smith, Ian Callaghan, Chris Lawler, Sammy Lee, David Fairclough all came through the system and survived. Steve has just set out on the journey."

A DEBUT GOAL

Steve Harkness also graduated to first-team football, and he acknowledged that his main problem was inexperience. At Carlisle he was a centre-forward, at Liverpool he dropped back to midfield, and then in the first team he played at full-back. "I'm putting that inexperience right with every game," he said.

Jamie Redknapp made his senior debut at Southampton, aged 18, and scored an equaliser, with his mum, brother and grand-dad looking on. His dad - Bournemouth manager Harry Redknapp - watched with pride too, as Jamie set up a goal for Dean Saunders against West Ham, the team for which Harry once played.

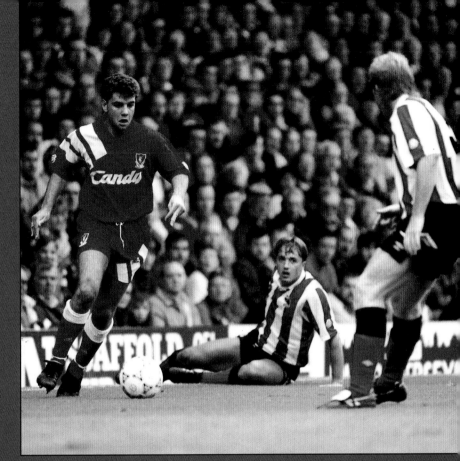

⚽ STEVE HARKNESS started his career as a striker at Carlisle, and the Sheffield Wednesday defence is in trouble as he goes forward.

⚽ STEVE McMANAMAN IS NOT AFRAID to take on players in international competition either. The Swarovski Tirol opponent dives at his feet in Austria.

49

APRIL - MAY

JOY AT LAST

RUSH

for

Liverpool may not have been in the title race in April, but they had a big say in who actually won it. And, of course, they went to Wembley to win the FA Cup final, after a dramatic semi-final against Portsmouth.

SOUNESS SHOCK

April opened with the semi-final against Portsmouth at Highbury and in a thrilling game, Ronnie Whelan snatched an equaliser with four minutes left in extra time. The whole football world was stunned, two days later, when it was announced that manager Graeme Souness was to undergo immediate open-heart surgery; Ronnie Moran, as he did in 1991, became the caretaker manager.

RONNY ROSENTHAL strikes home his goal in the 3-2 home defeat against Wimbledon.

RUSHY'S ATTEMPT on goal is foiled by John Lukic during the 0-0 draw against champions Leeds United.

In the League, Wimbledon won 3-2 at Anfield , while at Aston Villa a Tony Daley goal brought three home points. The FA Cup semi-final replay with Portsmouth followed and after 120 minutes of deadlock, penalties decided the issue; only Kit Symons scored for Pompey while Rush, Barnes and Saunders netted to send Liverpool to Wembley. In League action, Liverpool met Leeds at Anfield and drew 0-0; a trip to Highbury saw Arsenal administer a 4-0 hammering, and Ian Rush scored in the 1-1 draw at Nottingham Forest.

RUSHY'S DROUGHT ENDS

The last Sunday in April was crunch time. Leeds won their game to go four points clear and it meant that when Liverpool and Manchester United met at Anfield, Alex Ferguson's team had to win to stand any chance of taking the title. While United drove forward, it was Liverpool – and Ian Rush – who struck. Like Nicky Tanner, he didn't last the 90 minutes, but he had finally scored against Manchester United after 24 goalless appearances. Liverpool exploited United's loss of Gary Pallister in the closing minutes to score a second, Mark Walters following up a Ray Houghton shot which had been tipped against the crossbar by 'keeper Peter Schmeichel. This result left United runners up in the League to Leeds.

After a scoreless draw with third placed Sheffield Wednesday in their final League game, Liverpool went to Wembley intent on gaining a place in Europe as winners of the FA Cup, and after Sunderland had had their chances, Liverpool dominated the second half to emerge victorious, with goals from Thomas and Rush.

☼RESULTS☼

FOOTBALL LEAGUE 8 APRIL

LIVERPOOL 2	WIMBLEDON 3
Ronny Rosenthal	Lawrie Sanchez
Michael Thomas	Andy Clarke
	John Fashanu (Pen)

FOOTBALL LEAGUE 11 APRIL

ASTON VILLA 1	LIVERPOOL 0
Tony Daley	

FOOTBALL LEAGUE 18 APRIL

LIVERPOOL 0	LEEDS UNITED 0

FOOTBALL LEAGUE 20 APRIL

ARSENAL 4	LIVERPOOL 0
Ian Wright (2)	
David Hillier	
Anders Limpar	

FOOTBALL LEAGUE 22 APRIL

NOTTINGHAM FOREST 1	LIVERPOOL 1
Teddy Sheringham	Ian Rush

FOOTBALL LEAGUE 26 APRIL

LIVERPOOL 2	MANCHESTER
Ian Rush	UNITED 0
Mark Walters	

FOOTBALL LEAGUE 2 MAY

SHEFFIELD	LIVERPOOL 0
WEDNESDAY 0	

FINAL LEAGUE POSITION

Liverpool	P	W	D	L	F	A	Pts	Position
	42	16	16	10	47	40	64	Sixth

⚽ STEVE NICOL bursts through two would-be Nottingham Forest tacklers.

H e joined Liverpool after 18 months with Ayr United. Then manager, Bob Paisley rated Steve as: "one for the future." Steve has been at Anfield for ten years, and he rates Liverpool, "the best club in the country." His son, Michael, is glad he signed a new contract, too, because "he's football-daft and a Liverpool fan." Michael was club mascot when Sheffield United visited Anfield on New Year's Day, 1992.

They don't come any more versatile than Steve Nicol, and it is no wonder Liverpool manager Graeme Souness put him under contract until June, 1995. Steve said: "I'm delighted ... I cannot imagine myself playing for any other club. I hope to settle on Merseyside."

E V E R Y   R O L E

One way and another, Steve has played every role for Liverpool, bar two: "I've not kept goal, and never played at centre-forward. After all, the willingness to move about earned me my first selection in Liverpool's team. I played left-side midfield."

There was one occasion when he wore the goalkeeper's jersey, though that was in a cup semi-final for Ayr United Boys' Club, when their last line of defence was injured.

Steve Nicol

Nicky Tanner

BIG BREAK

Injuries were what gave the reserve-team centre-back Nicky Tanner his big break. Signed from Bristol Rovers for around £20,000, he seemed to be one of those players who wasn't quite going to make it at Anfield, where the demands are so great.

But during the three-month absence of Mark Wright, Nicky found himself being pitched into the fray and he became the team's last ever-present: "I was very pleased to get my chance, and I like to think I've taken it well. I felt when the new manager took over that everybody would be given a fair chance. I'm just grateful I've had this long run to prove what I can do." Nicky proved his point so well that he too was offered a new contract.

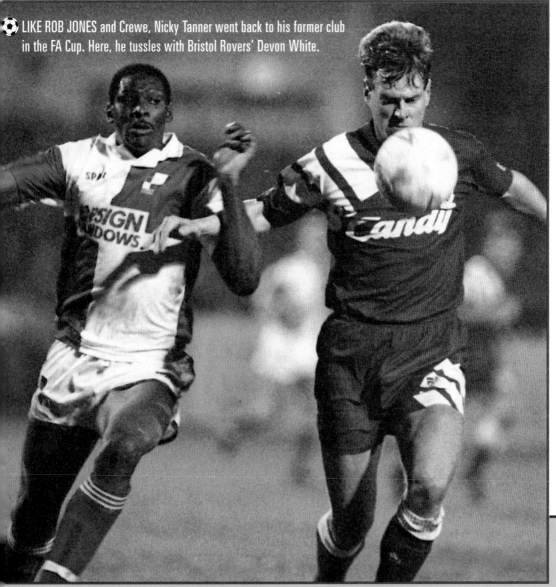

LIKE ROB JONES and Crewe, Nicky Tanner went back to his former club in the FA Cup. Here, he tussles with Bristol Rovers' Devon White.

a RAY of cheer

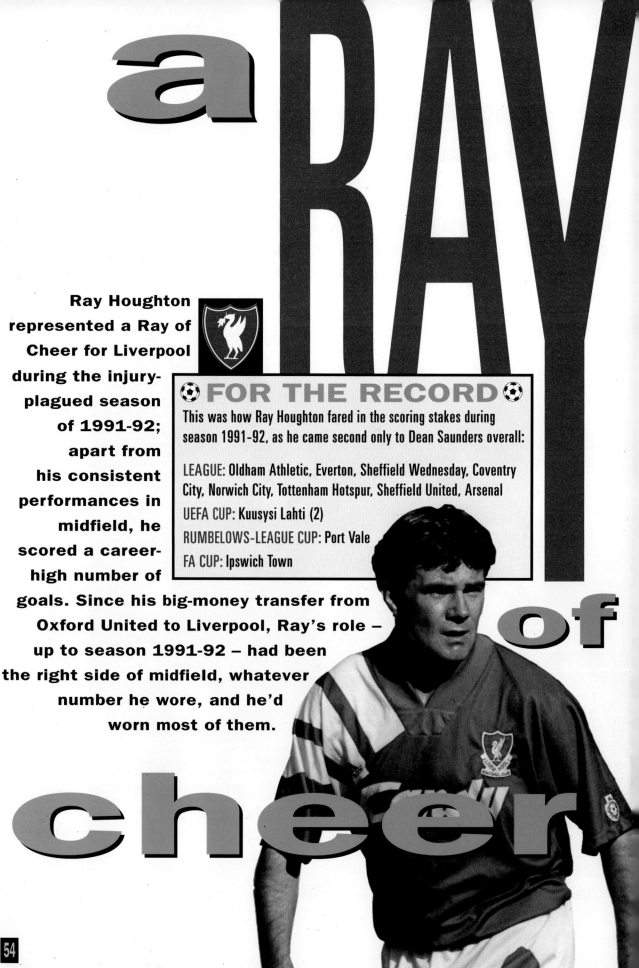

Ray Houghton represented a Ray of Cheer for Liverpool during the injury-plagued season of 1991-92; apart from his consistent performances in midfield, he scored a career-high number of goals. Since his big-money transfer from Oxford United to Liverpool, Ray's role – up to season 1991-92 – had been the right side of midfield, whatever number he wore, and he'd worn most of them.

⚽ FOR THE RECORD ⚽

This was how Ray Houghton fared in the scoring stakes during season 1991-92, as he came second only to Dean Saunders overall:

LEAGUE: Oldham Athletic, Everton, Sheffield Wednesday, Coventry City, Norwich City, Tottenham Hotspur, Sheffield United, Arsenal

UEFA CUP: Kuusysi Lahti (2)

RUMBELOWS-LEAGUE CUP: Port Vale

FA CUP: Ipswich Town

But Liverpool's injury problems meant Ray took on a different role as he switched from wide on the right to an inside spot in midfield, at the same time showing that he was capable of getting his name on the scoresheet on a regular basis. Ray had recognised, soon after he joined Liverpool, that he should be scoring more goals, season by season.

STUDIED VIDEOS

He began to study videos, to work out the art of scoring goals from a midfield position, paying special attention to the positioning and timing of runs by players who were recognised as midfield marksmen. Two things struck him, as he watched the videos. Ray summed it up: "I wasn't in the penalty area often enough to score goals; and on the few occasions when I did get into the box, the timing of my runs was wrong. I wasn't in the right position at the right time."

The result of his deliberations? "I've made a big effort to get into the box more often, and I'm pleased to be able to report that all my goals have come from close in." But he added: "Ideally, I'd like to keep up the close-in stuff, and add a few goals from outside the area as well."

RAY HOUGHTON acknowledges another goal; his celebrations aren't flashy, but who cares? What counts is that the ball is in the net!.

SHEFFIELD UNITED 'keeper, Simon Tracey, is at full stretch to keep out this Houghton effort in the New Year's Day game at Anfield.

Liverpool's first European jaunt, after a six-year absence, ended disappointingly at the quarter-final stage but, along the way, they overcame opposition from Finland, France and Austria before losing to Genoa, who joined Ferencvaros and Red Star Belgrade as the only clubs to defeat the Anfield Reds in both legs.

BACK IN EUROPE, AND NOW HERE'S TO NEXT TIME

⚽ ON THE FLIGHT to Finland for the second leg, manager Graeme Souness cuts the cake that says it all: "Welcome back to Europe."

⚽ RESULTS ⚽

FIRST ROUND, FIRST LEG 18 SEPTEMBER

LIVERPOOL 6	KUUSYSI LAHTI 1
Dean Saunders (4)	Kalie Lehtinen
Ray Houghton (2)	

FIRST ROUND, SECOND LEG 2 OCTOBER

KUUSYSI LAHTI 1	LIVERPOOL 0
Mike Belfield	

SECOND ROUND, FIRST LEG 23 OCTOBER

AUXERRE 2	LIVERPOOL 0
Jean-Marc Ferreri	
Kalman Kovacs	

SECOND ROUND, SECOND LEG 6 NOVEMBER

LIVERPOOL 3	AUXERRE 0
Jan Molby (pen)	
Mike Marsh	
Mark Walters	

THIRD ROUND, FIRST LEG 27 NOVEMBER

SWAROVSKI TIROL 0	LIVERPOOL 2
	Dean Saunders (2)

THIRD ROUND, SECOND LEG 11 DECEMBER

LIVERPOOL 4	SWAROVSKI TIROL 0
Dean Saunders (3)	
Barry Venison	

FOURTH ROUND, FIRST LEG 4 MARCH

GENOA 2	LIVERPOOL 0
Valeriano Fiorin	
Branco	

FOURTH ROUND, SECOND LEG 18 MARCH

LIVERPOOL 1	GENOA 2
Ian Rush	Carlos Aguilera

⚽ JAMIE REDKNAPP becomes Liverpool's youngest-ever player in a European match when he played in the first leg against Auxerre.

Dean Saunders and Jamie Redknapp had cause for personal satisfaction: Dean's nine goals in three European matches is a new club record; and Jamie, when he played against Auxerre in France at the age of 18 years and four months, became the youngest-ever Liverpool player in European competition.

Liverpool started with a tie against Kuusysi Lahti. The Reds hosted the first leg and won, 6-1, Dean Saunders (4), Ray Houghton (2) – both making their European debuts – scoring. The return game provided a shock, because the Finns won, 1-0, but the Reds cruised into the next round. The second round first leg saw Liverpool crash, 2-0, at Auxerre in France, and when the teams met for the Anfield leg, manager Graeme Souness urged the home fans to support their team all the way.

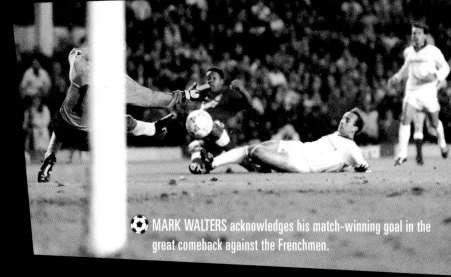

⚽ MARK WALTERS acknowledges his match-winning goal in the great comeback against the Frenchmen.

GREAT FIGHT BACK

They did just that, and they were rewarded. An early Jan Molby penalty set the scene; then man-of-the-match, Mike Marsh scored; and finally, a stunning strike by Mark Walters gave Liverpool victory, 3-2 on aggregate. Austrians, Swarovski Tirol, were third round opponents and, in the away leg, Dean Saunders struck twice in a 2-0 stroll. At Anfield, Liverpool hit four; Deano netting his second Euro hat-trick, and substitute Barry Venison scoring his first-ever European goal. Liverpool faced Genoa in the quarter-finals, and the away leg ended ominously, as Genoa scored a late goal to make it 2-0 on the night.

NOT THIS TIME

Try as they might, Liverpool could not do to Genoa what they had done to Auxerre. The Italians scored first again, and though Ian Rush equalised soon after the restart, Genoa got another. So the Reds went out, beaten 4-1 on aggregate. But if Liverpool lost, they could be proud of the way their team performed.

The long and winding road to

CREWE ALEXANDRA

Liverpool's quest for a fifth FA Cup began at Crewe in the third round. Nerves following the Peterborough defeat were erased by an early Steve McManaman goal and by John Barnes, back after missing 32 games, who notched a hat-trick. Graeme Souness summed up: "We've missed Barnes, any team would. I hope it's a turning point for us."

The next round brought a trip to Twerton Park, Bath, and Second Division Bristol Rovers. The game ended 1-1, with Dean Saunders putting Liverpool ahead, only for Rovers' Saunders — Carl — to equalise.

BIRTHDAY JOY FOR STEVE

At Anfield, Carl Saunders struck a spectacular goal to give the West-Countrymen the lead. Then, on his 20th birthday, Steve McManaman rescued Liverpool. Early in the second half he scored a stunning equaliser; and with 13 minutes left, he raced 75 yards to create the winner for Dean Saunders. Steve said of his goal: "I'll always remember it. It's one of my best ." Second Division champions-elect Ipswich Town were waiting for Liverpool, and the home team had ex-Anfield Red John Wark at the heart of their defence. He came closest to scoring, heading a corner against the Liverpool bar. After 90 minutes it was 0-0, and back to Anfield for the replay.

CROCKS OF GOLD

Ipswich took the game to Liverpool, and the match was decided in extra time. Jan Molby, Ray Houghton, Steve Nicol and Rob Jones played though not fully fit, and Liverpool finally won, 3-2. Houghton and Molby both scored, with Steve McManaman settling the issue. Houghton put the Reds ahead; Molby drove home a stunning free-kick in extra-time; and McManaman struck soon after. The quarter-final brought Aston Villa to Anfield, with ex-Red Steve Staunton in their team. Graeme Souness recalled Ronnie Whelan, after his knee operations and two reserve games; John Barnes, out for seven weeks; and Michael Thomas, absent for five weeks, and with only a few days' training.

The gamble paid off when, with 20 minutes to go, Whelan passed to Barnes, who set up Thomas, and he struck a sweet shot past 'keeper Nigel Spink, for the game's only goal. Immediately after the Villa match the draw for the semi-finals was made, and Liverpool were paired with Portsmouth at Highbury on Sunday, April 5. Portsmouth took the lead early in the second period of extra time through Darren Anderton, but as the minutes ticked away Liverpool stormed forward and Steve Nicol was brought down. John Barnes struck a curling free kick from 20 yards out, the ball rebounded off the inside of the post, and fell invitingly for Ronnie Whelan to tap home. ▶

WEMBLEY

With Liverpool manager Graeme Souness in hospital following his open-heart surgery, Ronnie Moran took over for the Villa Park replay, though Souness directed team

Saunders put Liverpool 3-1 up, which meant Andy Awford knew he had to score to keep the match alive. But, like Kuhl, the Portsmouth defender dragged his shot wide. It

► MICHAEL THOMAS wins an aerial duel in the first semi-final game.

AS JOHN BARNES Strikes a free kick, Ronnie Whelan (5) starts his run; before any Portsmouth player could react to the rebound from the post Whelan scored the equaliser.

selection. Portsmouth came closest to scoring in the replay, a shot which struck the bar, but it came down to a penalty shoot-out, with Pompey being the first to try their luck.

SPOT THE BALL

Portsmouth skipper Martin Kuhl took aim, but as Bruce Grobbelaar went to his right, he drove the ball wide of the opposite post. Up stepped John Barnes, and he coolly beat Alan Knight; then it was the turn of Kit Symons, and he made the scoreline 1-1. Ian Rush's aim was true and he too scored. Warren Neill was next, and his shot was held by Grobbelaar, who this time had stood his ground in the middle of the goal. Dean

was all over; Graeme Souness celebrated with champagne in his hospital room.

To get to Wembley in 1992, Second Division Sunderland had beaten Port Vale, Oxford United, West Ham (after a replay), Chelsea (also at the second attempt) and Norwich City in a scrappy semi-final, striker John Byrne scoring in every round.

ASTON VILLA

PORTSMOUTH

⚽ IAN RUSH turns away after netting in the semi-final at Highbury, only for the goal to be disallowed for offside.

WEMBLEY

FA CUP REPORT 2

⚽RESULTS⚽

THIRD ROUND 6 JANUARY	
CREWE ALEXANDRA 0	LIVERPOOL 4
	Steve McManaman
	John Barnes (3-1 Pen)

FOURTH ROUND 5 FEBRUARY	
BRISTOL ROVERS 1	LIVERPOOL 1
Carl Saunders	Dean Saunders

FOURTH ROUND REPLAY 11 FEBRUARY	
LIVERPOOL 2	BRISTOL ROVERS 1
Steve McManaman	Carl Saunders
Dean Saunders	

FIFTH ROUND 16 FEBRUARY	
IPSWICH TOWN 0	LIVERPOOL 0

FIFTH ROUND REPLAY 26 FEBRUARY	
LIVERPOOL 3	IPSWICH TOWN 2
Ray Houghton	Gavin Johnson
Jan Molby	Jason Dozzell
Steve McManaman	

SIXTH ROUND 8 MARCH	
LIVERPOOL 1	ASTON VILLA 0
Michael Thomas	

SEMI-FINAL 5 APRIL	
LIVERPOOL 1	PORTSMOUTH 1
Ronnie Whelan	Darren Anderton

SEMI-FINAL REPLAY 13 APRIL	
LIVERPOOL 0	PORTSMOUTH 0
(Liverpool won 3-1 after Penalties)	
John Barnes	Kit Symons
Ian Rush	
Dean Saunders	

FA CUP REPORT FINAL

⚽ RESULT ⚽

9 MAY

LIVERPOOL 2	SUNDERLAND 0
Michael Thomas	
Ian Rush	

Liverpool were without John Barnes and Ronnie Whelan at Wembley, but bolstered by the return of Steve McManaman. Another boost was the appearance of Graeme Souness, 24 hours after his release from hospital, although Ronnie Moran led the team out.

⚽ **LEFT:** MICHAEL THOMAS strikes brilliantly on the volley to give Liverpool the lead shortly after half-time.

⚽ **FAR RIGHT:** LIVERPOOL'S second is on it's way via the clinical boot of Ian Rush.

The Flo

Michael Thomas almost scored in the first two minutes, but Sunderland came into it; John Byrne missed a good chance; Bruce Grobbelaar cracked his head against an upright saving from Anton Rogan, and Mark Wright deflected another goalbound effort away.

THOMAS REPAYS A DEBT

Late in the half Steve McManaman switched flanks, from left to right, and this proved to be a match-winning move. He was brought down by Paul Bracewell on the stroke of half-time, but a penalty surprisingly was not awarded. Then, in the 47th minute, surrounded by two defenders, he flicked the ball to Michael Thomas who sent a superb volley past Tony Norman.

RECORD-BREAKER RUSH

As Thomas made up for his 1989 goal which deprived Liverpool of the championship, so Ian Rush set a record, scoring his fifth Wembley Cup-final goal, latching on to a Thomas pass and curling a low shot beyond Norman into the far corner. That goal knocked the heart out of Sunderland and Liverpool took command, with Jan Molby orchestrating proceedings. Dean Saunders could have had at least one goal, Tony

Norman made a number of saves, and Sunderland just chased shadows; at one stage the Reds made 12 passes without a Sunderland player getting near the ball.

On the final whistle Mark Wright collected the Cup and it was passed from player to player, before the team did a lap of honour, knowing they would compete in the European Cup-winners Cup next season.

Final

⚽ **RONNIE MORAN,** Graeme Souness and Roy Evans parade Liverpool's fifth FA Cup trophy.

urish...

ROLL OF HONOUR

FOOTBALL LEAGUE CHAMPIONS

1900-01	1976-77
1905-06	1978-79
1921-22	1979-80
1922-23	1981-82
1946-47	1982-83
1963-64	1983-84
1965-66	1985-86
1972-73	1987-88
1975-76	1989-90

FA CUP WINNERS

1964-65
1973-74
1985-86
1988-89
1991-92

EUROPEAN CUP WINNERS

1976-77
1977-78
1980-81
1983-84

UEFA CUP WINNERS

1972-73
1975-76

LEAGUE/MILK CUP WINNERS

1980-81
1981-82
1982-83
1983-84